FROM SEED
TO APPLE

---

*Inspirational stories & lessons learned
from Washington's 2019 Teachers of the Year*

Volume IX
2019

From Seed to Apple is a publication of the Washington Teacher of the Year program and Washington Teacher Advisory Council (WATAC), which are administered by the Office of Superintendent of Public Instruction (OSPI). Teacher of the Year and WATAC are partially funded by private donations including a grant from the Bill & Melinda Gates Foundation. The Teachers of the Year and members of WATAC speak with independent voices. Their opinions, beliefs, and viewpoints do not necessarily reflect, nor are they influenced by, the state superintendent or donors.

The names of all students featured in this volume have been changed.

A digital version of this publication is available for download at **bit.ly/FromSeedToApple**.

Subscribe for updates at **bit.ly/SeedToAppleUpdates**.

*To our students and their stories.
They inspire us every day to
understand, empower, and elevate
their messages.*

Table of Contents

Mandy Manning
2018 Washington State and National
Teacher of the Year

Joel E. Ferris High School
Spokane School District

Foreword

Messages matter. After nearly 20 years in the classroom, this is the most important lesson I've learned. In every interaction we have with our students, our colleagues, and out in the world with our communities, we send messages — not only with our words, but with our actions. We are communicating how we feel and what we believe or perceive about each individual who comes into our lives. That's powerful.

As a Teacher of the Year, this idea has become even more crystallized during my travel from community to community and school to school. I've met with educators, education advocates, and students across the state. I've had the privilege of witnessing the wonderful work happening in our classrooms and the impacts of amazing teachers on their students. The importance of our messages is never more clear than when I observe an interaction between a student and a teacher who obviously believes in them, or I see the notes of appreciation from students pinned across the walls of a classroom.

What we say matters, and how we send those messages matters even more — especially when we are in positions of power. We can empower or destroy a young person in a single interaction. I know this from my own experiences as an educator, both good and bad. I also know this from being a student. One teacher's message destroyed my confidence in my ability to do math, and another teacher's consistent message of belief encouraged me to become a confident and focused young woman, ready to take on the world.

The educators whose personal and transformative stories fill the following pages understand that messages matter. They carry the mantel of teacher with honor and responsibility, and they know that every interaction with their students carries tremendous weight. Most importantly, they understand that the classroom is not simply a place of learning. It is a place of growth and identity. Educators, all adults really, have the power to unlock potential and empower kids to believe in themselves.

As you read these stories, these glimpses into the tireless commitment of teachers to their students, I hope you (like me) are moved. Moved by the power of these educators' messages. Most of all, moved to be better. To take care with our words and our actions, because our messages change lives.

Mathew Brown
North Central ESD 171 Regional Teacher of the Year

Manson Middle School and Manson High School
Manson School District

The Power of Positivity

*Believing in the potential of students
transforms a small-town band program*

I teach 6th–12th-grade band, choir, jazz, and sometimes a guitar and piano class in the town of Manson on Lake Chelan — a beautiful resort area in north central Washington. Manson is very much a small town. There are no roads that go past Manson, and to go any further up the 50-mile-long and 26th deepest lake in the world, a person must either take a boat or hike.

I grew up and learned to be a teacher in large schools. I am a proud graduate of Inglemoor High School, a school that year after year has 400 or more students in each graduating class. While student teaching for the music department of the University of Washington, I was placed at Mercer Island Middle School and High School directing bands with four amazing mentor teachers. Their music program was so well supported that they could spell out M-E-R-C-E-R I-S-L-A-N-D with their marching tubas and even add a space. That is 13 tubas!

When I came to Manson, my first teaching job, it was a culture shock. The graduating class each year ranged from 35 to 55 students, the student population was 70 percent free and reduced lunch, and the entire district was only 600 students. The tuba section of our marching band spelled M-A. I was the only music teacher, and I needed a plan.

My first year we had 18 students in the high school band, a far cry from what I had ever experienced. But I decided to go with what I knew, giving my students music that was as complex as I had played or taught at Mercer Island.

It was a disaster. Not only was it a challenge to teach the students the complex rhythms and difficult notes, but we didn't even have all the instruments necessary to make the music sound good.

At this point, there were three possible roads to take:

1. Keep doing the same thing, and blame the students for never practicing.

2. Give up.

3. Evaluate where the students were, and help them to build their skills.

Though I eventually came to the belief that the latter was the way to go, it took me a few years. I made many mistakes, but in the end decided to stay positive and persevere. Eventually I started to see that every student had a place in the music program. The focus of the program went from earning trophies to ensuring that the students in my program would love music regardless of their ability. My goal was to reach everyone.

In my fourth year of teaching, Hector tested this belief. Hector was a senior who had just moved into our small town. He was a rough and tumble kid, he had never played an instrument before, but for some reason he wanted to join band. While I could have turned him away to a class where he wouldn't struggle as much, I chose to take him on. We worked hard to help him catch up to his peers. I made a choice early on to focus on the things that he was doing well as opposed to his mistakes. Through his own perseverance and belief in himself, he became the band's lead trumpet player in just one year. To this day, the memory of his success continues to motivate me to believe in every student.

As the band grew, I took stock of the instruments the school district owned and realized we needed more. After talking with my superintendent, we decided to write a press release asking the community how they would like to support their music program. They could donate any unused instruments, money, or their time by volunteering. By the next week, the *Wenatchee World*, the largest newspaper in our region, had picked up our story and put it on the front page. Within a day of its release, we had donations from places within a 100-mile radius. That year, because of the positive vision we had for our program, we were able to serve 150 students in the music program!

The Manson music program now serves over 90 percent of the middle school and a third of the students in the high school from year to year. We have three marching tubas and can spell M-I-I-S when we march in parades. All students — regardless of socio-economic status, race, language acquisition, or ability — can pursue their musical dreams. Our students are driven to succeed and inspired to always push their own limits. They know that everyone has potential and will be allowed to follow their own musical journey.

The huge game changer in my career has been a positive outlook. In our education system, there should be no failures. There is and always will be growth potential. When we look at it through this lens, we will find positive solutions to any challenge. In the symphony of life, we all have a melody. We just need to learn how to sing it. That is why teaching is so important. We help our students to find their voices. As educators, we make a difference when we believe every student in our classroom can make it to the final note.

Karen Doran
Olympic ESD 114 Regional Teacher of the Year

Roosevelt Elementary
Port Angeles School District

Champions for Children

When students experience trauma, adult mentors can make all the difference

As a teacher, I have learned there are two kinds of things students bring to class. There are the things students fill their backpacks with that bring excitement to the start of a new year. And then there are the things that fill their minds, shaping and molding them into productive students and community members. Through my years of teaching, I have seen firsthand how students are affected by the events in their lives. These events have a profound impact on their ability to learn and function in the classroom. As I start each year, I wonder, what are my students' stories? How have their stories shaped their lives? How will their stories affect their ability to be successful in my class? The stories of their lives are what shape our classroom. For it is their stories that affect our classroom, designing and influencing our yearly learning experience.

Some childhood experiences cause extreme toxic stress and affect both the physical and mental abilities of children and adults alike. These experiences are commonly known as Adverse Childhood Experiences (ACEs). ACEs have a profound and negative impact on a child's ability to learn, build relationships, and make positive connections with others. This is the story of a 5th-grade girl, a story seldom told but often heard. A story that, through no fault of her own, shaped her and molded her into the classroom teacher she is today. It is a story of tragedy, a story of love, and a story of resiliency. It is my story.

GRRR. The alarm went off louder and earlier every morning once the school year started, or at least that is what it felt like. Living in rural America, for a preteen, was no easy task. "Up before the chickens," is what Grandpa would say, and "Early bird gets the worm." Mom was already gone by the time I pulled my head from the pillow. A shower and breakfast would not happen again this morning because there was no time. My ride to school would be here in five minutes. Knowing I had to hurry to catch the bus, lunch would be, again, an unlabeled can Mom picked up the week before from her grocery store job. Mom worked in the evenings at Bag and Save after finishing her full-time job delivering mail.

My sister was a year older, but it never really felt like it. We were a fluke of nature, Mom would say, "Two babies in one year doesn't happen naturally unless you're a rabbit." My sister was born in January, and I showed up in December of the same year. The picture hanging in Mom's room was evidence that I once had an older brother. In the picture, I was propped up next to him as we both smiled wildly for the camera. His first pair of shoes, dipped in bronze, sat at the base of the picture. The picture was the only evidence of my older brother. Why he was not with us was a mystery to me for years. It was not until much later in life that I came to realize why it was important not to talk about his absence; the pain and grief was too much for my mother to bear.

School! It was time for school and I needed to find my homework before I headed out the door to get on the bus. Looking for my homework was like looking for a needle in a haystack. Not sure why it was so important to look for it because, once again, I didn't have time to get it done. Mom had gotten home late, and I was too busy riding my horse and playing outside to get much of anything done. Well, let's be honest — I didn't have a clue about how to do the math. And since the story we were reading in class was of no interest to me, I figured why bother?

I tried to explain to my teacher that I had meant to get my homework done. I just didn't have the time. My excuse would fall on deaf ears as she reminded me that I would need to stay in for recess to get caught up. There was nothing worse than staying in to work on spelling and reading when all I really wanted to do was hang out with my friend, the one person that understood me. I would work at my desk while my teacher would refill her coffee cup, visit with the other teachers, and use the restroom. Recess would come to an end. The blank page, left from the night before, would still be staring back at me. I would be reminded that I needed to "try harder" to get the work done. And maybe one more recess trapped inside might help me finish the work. I was intuitive enough to read between the lines and my teacher's sarcasm, and it cut like a knife. I had let one more person down in my life. A feeling of defeat and despair filled my mind.

School was never easy. I always wanted to do well but could never pull it together. I knew I just needed to make it to the 12th grade, and I would be done. "No more recess. No more books. No more teacher's dirty looks!" The song echoes through my brain even today. Mom had made it clear, "No college for the two of you girls. I can't afford it, and your dad…he has never helped." Mom rarely said that word: D-A-D. It felt like a curse word. I think I was nearly an adult before I said it.

My parents' divorce was inevitable after they lost their oldest child (my brother) in a tragic accident on the family farm. When my dad took his anger out on Mom, Grandpa made sure he never came around again. After that, Dad would spend time in and out of jail on violence and drug related charges. I think I was in 5th grade when Mom took us to see him for the first time since he had left all those years ago. I left that visit paralyzed with fear and sure that she had made a mistake; that man could not be my father!

Schoolwork was not the only thing that was a challenge for me; relationships were also difficult. I figured out early that one way I could get praise from my teachers was by not talking. I often could go all day without uttering a word to a single person. I was always seated next to the most talkative people in the class. To my mother at parent teacher conferences, my teacher would praise my ability to refrain from talking. My inability to strike up a conversation and build a relationship was seen as an asset. What I know now is this was both a blessing and a curse. The trauma I had experienced in my childhood kept me silent in class and impacted my ability to build relationships. Childhood trauma would continue to have a lasting impact on my life for years to come.

The weekends held uncertainty for me. It felt like every weekend was a party. Mom would invite friends over Saturday night and most of them wouldn't leave until

Sunday afternoon. For the most part, they seemed to be fun parties. The adults would drink and smoke while the kids played outside. Most of the adults I would see again the following weekend, but I never knew who they really were.

As I headed into middle school, a new mix of students filled the room, and the feelings I was having felt foreign. My unpreparedness for the flood of hormones and high-risk childhood experiences left me ill-prepared for what would happen to me in the years to come. Middle school would find me head over heels for the class troublemaker. He had been kicked out of his previous school for fighting, and there was something so intriguing about that to me. By the beginning of high school, we were inseparable. Needless to say, I would find myself a young mother at age 17. I would have two more children over the next three years. As predicted by statistics, I would also leave and start a new life for my own safety and the safety of my children. The resulting disappointment I brought my mother was a pain I regretted and internalized for years. As a mother myself, I now know my mother spent most of her young adulthood in survival mode. She did her best in spite of the circumstances that challenged her ability to be the parent she dreamed of being. I too dreamed of raising my children in an environment where they could thrive. Still, I found myself in a situation where I could not hold my head high and be proud of my decisions. Instead, my actions brought me shame, which is so often the case for victims.

ACEs have a devastating effect on our children and society, but there is hope. Rita Pierson, a lifelong educator and child advocate, asserts, "Every child deserves a champion: an adult who will never give up on them, who understands

---

the power of connections and insists they become the best they can be." Every child deserves a champion.

What I needed was someone to walk alongside me and be my champion. That champion ended up being my aunt. At my darkest hour she told me I could go to college. I could be and do whatever I wanted. She gave me hope and willingly supported my family and me as I worked my way through my first semester of college. With the continued support from my aunt and mother, I completed my degree at the University of New Mexico and eventually became a teacher. I stand here today, proud of the work I have done both in and out of the classroom.

Adverse Childhood Experiences cause toxic stress. Statistics say 67 percent of adults have at least one ACE. Higher ACE scores also mean a student is more likely to have physical, mental, and emotional difficulties. With an ACE score of 5 or higher, students are at a severe disadvantage and will find it very difficult to function in the classroom. They need extra support to learn, build relationships, and communicate effectively. That said, I am proof that ACEs do not define us! They are obstacles, but we can overcome them.

As a teacher and supporter of children, I've become more aware of the opportunities adults have to support children. It starts with recognizing the needs of the children in our lives, helping them strengthen the characteristics necessary for perseverance and resilience. Become a mentor, build and strengthen community partnerships, volunteer your expertise. Provide the stability children need emotionally and educationally.

Every child has a story. A story that shapes and molds them into who they are today and who they will be in the future.

Help write the story of a child in your class, your church, your family, or your community. Provide stability, support resiliency, and infuse his or her story with compassion and hope. Be the champion in that one child's life, and make a difference.

Kimberly Miller
ESD 112 Regional Teacher of the Year

Woodland High School
Woodland School District

Stuck on the Fence

*When adults tolerate bullying,
the consequences are devastating
for students*

I have often pondered what it is that marks one student as a target for bullying. Once the harassment starts, it is almost as if the bullies are sharks scenting fresh blood. They return to the same child over and over. I have seen adorable, well-groomed children chosen, but most often those who are different seem to be at higher risk of becoming the target. These are children who may be a bit socially awkward; often they are very kind and soft-hearted children. Some victims are shy and quiet. Others are a little slow to understand teasing and facial expressions. This was the case with Caleb.

Caleb was a loving, kind boy who would run up and hug strangers because he enjoyed people so much. He was full of laughter and joy; he loved animals and make-believe stories. But Caleb was slow to read people's expressions, and he didn't understand when people teased him.

By the time Caleb entered 2nd grade, he was often alone at school, students asked him over less often, and he was not included in social outings with the other children. Unfortunately, personal interaction was one area in which he still struggled. His lack of understanding teasing led students to tease him even more. He didn't understand why they were making fun of him, and he began to react with anger. His classmates enjoyed seeing him get angry, and the bullying got worse; his personality started to change. The once happy go lucky boy, who enjoyed people so much, started to lash out at people.

Caleb became depressed and surly, closing himself off rather than dealing with people. At the same time, it became apparent that he was very intelligent, quick to pick up math and science concepts. Caleb's strength in math and science led to him being placed in the highly capable program. This could have been a wonderful time to engage his very academic mind. Unfortunately, it simply led to extra worksheets and was another way he was different. He was now bullied and harassed for being smart.

By 3rd grade, Caleb was acting out in the classroom in order to make the taunting and harassment stop. He didn't trust many people, including his teacher who was aware of the bullying, but did nothing to stop it. It was at this time that the bullying became physical. His mother worked in a nearby school, and Caleb would walk to her work at the end of the school day. One day she received a call from a staff member that her son was caught on the fence surrounding the football field. It turned out some of the boys from his class had followed him that day. They were taunting him and throwing rocks at him. He couldn't outrun them, so he decided to climb the fence to get away from them. As he went over the fence his shirt got caught;

he was stuck hanging there three feet from the ground. Caleb was hurt, scared, and angry, sobbing about how the kids treated him.

His family moved him to a different school, and he had an amazing group of teachers and administrators who worked with him to change the way he handled teasing. The many hours, coping strategies, and kindness they put toward this traumatized child made it possible for him to turn a corner and start changing that cycle of being bullied and acting out. It took many years and many behavior plans, as well as conferences and mental health counseling, to make a difference in his learned behaviors. In some ways, Caleb was lucky; he ended up with teachers who wouldn't tolerate the harassment, bullying, and intimidation that had gone on before. They recognized there was still a kind and loving person inside this angry young man.

As parents, we trust our schools to keep our children safe. We expect teachers will teach about accepting all students, and that the child we love so much, will be loved by others and have a wonderful experience in school. But this isn't always the case. I know because Caleb is my child.

Every day in schools across the country we have students dealing with this issue, and families struggling to mitigate the deep harm caused by bullying. It is time to bring more training into our schools and communities to recognize the red flag behaviors exhibited by bullies and victims alike. We need to bring more mental health counselors into our schools and provide resources for parents to learn about bullying and ways to stop it early. We need to help the children already traumatized to learn coping behaviors. We need to recognize that children do not always speak up when they are bullied. They are often not sure people will believe them. They may be embarrassed or afraid of reprisals.

Adults should look for the warning signs:

- Behavior changes
- Unexplained injuries
- Loss of friends or social life
- Lack of interest or turning inwards
- Difficulty sleeping
- Not wanting to go to school
- Feelings of helplessness
- Decreased self-esteem

If you see any of the signs or symptoms, please speak up. As educators, we are the first line of defense for these children. It is our job to step in and put a stop to bullying and teach our children and communities it must not be tolerated.

Tracy Castro-Gill
Puget Sound ESD 121 Regional Teacher of the Year

Seattle School District

Those Times They Tried to Bury Me

And how I help seeds grow

I am a teacher activist. This wasn't always the case. I had this idea that as a woman of color who experienced poverty and domestic and substance abuse, my presence alone would be enough to motivate my students of color and students experiencing poverty and trauma. That was a wrong assumption. I quickly learned that my experiences didn't matter as much as the way I presented in the classroom.

I am the daughter of Richard Castro and Rita Hust. My father is Mexican-American, and my mother is generically white. The story is that she's German and Dutch, but she feels no connection to either culture. Both of my parents grew up in a suburb of Los Angeles with a large Mexican-American population, and it's the same place I grew up. For most of my childhood, my family experienced poverty. My parents were teenage parents, and I'm their first born. Despite my dad's exceptional work ethic, we lived in subsidized housing and received welfare benefits in the form of Medicaid and periodic assistance from our church for food and rent until I was well into my high school career.

My father's father decided not to teach his children to speak Spanish even though he continues to speak it fluently. He believed it would be in their best interest, during a time in which it was illegal to speak Spanish in California schools, for his kids to only speak English. This was no longer the case in the 1980s when I started to go to school. This meant that, I, Tracy Castro, with brown skin, stuck out like a sore thumb in my Mexican-American community where nearly all of my peers spoke at least broken Spanish. I did not. My mixed-race identity and inability to speak Spanish in a Spanish-speaking community left me in a cultural and racial limbo. I was too white for some of my Brown peers and not white enough for many of my white peers.

As I began to explore my identity in my teens, I found the majority of my Mexican-American peers were involved in things like ditching school, getting high, and gang activity. I didn't necessarily want to be a part of those things, but I wanted to feel like I was a part of "being" Mexican-American. Even though my family at home told me I was "just American," that never resonated with me because my teachers and peers saw me as Mexican-American. Even my Chicanx peers acknowledged it as they rejected me. "You're a traitor to La Raza," they would say to me if I refused to join their gang. I remember having a conversation with my Chicanx peers about what Mexican-American culture even meant. My peers decided gang and prison culture were Mexican-American culture. I argued against that, but what did I know? I didn't even speak Spanish. Eventually, I broke down and began to be part of that life.

During my junior year of high school, I became pregnant. At that point, I was behind in credits and on the verge of dropping out. I enrolled in an alternative school and gave birth to my first son in January of my senior year. I became pregnant with my second son a few months later. This was the beginning of decades of poverty and domestic abuse despite managing to graduate high school early with a baby and one on the way. I went to college off and on and received an associate degree eight years after graduating high school. Seven years later, and about 15 years into my abusive marriage, I went to university where I took my first Ethnic Studies course. This was life-changing for me. I understood for the first time that had my grandfather not felt the need to assimilate into white culture, my life may have turned out so differently. I was going to college with the intent of becoming a teacher, but it was then I knew I would be an Ethnic Studies teacher.

My experiences with abuse and poverty are never visible in the classroom, especially considering that teachers are seen as middle-class success stories. Many students see teachers as loaded. Most kids knew I wasn't white. Some kids guessed I'm Mexican, and others have told me they thought, "Oh great, another white teacher." The kids who saw me as Mexican were almost always Latinx themselves. They would tentatively ask, "You're Mexican, right?" I would confirm their assumption, and they would laugh and turn to a friend and say, "See? I knew it!" I was saddened that I was considered a novelty because they weren't used to seeing people like them at the front of the class This affirmed for me, however, the need not only for more educators of color, but for an Ethnic Studies curriculum that is more representative of the students we teach.

Those initial experiences of being seen as a novelty occurred while I was substitute teaching in a district with a predominantly Latinx student population. When I was assigned my first full-time teaching position, I was in a school that had recently undergone a boundary change that resulted in an influx of Black and Pacific Islander students into a school whose student population and teaching staff were very white. I went in knowing my focus would be ethnic studies and racial justice. I taught Washington State History and English Language Arts to 7th graders. The time I spent at the school was insightful and the beginning of an awakening for me. I was a first-year teacher whose students were performing for me on levels that impressed the veteran teachers in the building. Students of color were asking to be transferred into my class, but I don't think it's because I was a "better teacher." I honestly believe it was because I was an "honest teacher" who spoke to their lived experiences and who trusted them with content others thought was above their heads. Many white people are uncomfortable and ill-equipped to address racial oppression, so they assume students will also be uncomfortable or ill-equipped.

I remember teaching a lesson to commemorate Martin Luther King, Jr. Day. I wanted to be purposeful about going deeper than the superficial, "Yay! Racism is over thanks to Dr. King's I Have a Dream Speech!" My lesson was on the history of Black resistance and liberation and the historic events and circumstances that required the activism of Dr. King and his generation of activists. I highlighted activists like Frederick Douglass and Ida B. Wells. I taught them about the Black resistance movement during the Jim Crow era, focusing on how Black Americans didn't just accept their oppression as history portrays. My lesson was powerful for the students, but also for me in cementing my commitment to ethnic studies because absolutely none of my students had ever heard this story. One Black student said, "You mean there were civil rights leaders before Dr. King?"

In my second year of teaching I was assigned to teach 6th-grade Ancient World History. I thought, "Great... how am I going to teach Ethnic Studies?" Luckily, I was also assigned to the best teaching partner I could have asked for, Andrew Chase. I've compared our working relationship and pedagogical philosophies as peanut butter and jelly — great separately and perfect together. Together we were able to build an entire year of Ancient World History Ethnic Studies! It took some time to get it to what it ended up being, and I couldn't be prouder of the work we did together.

Andrew and I were able to make ancient world history relevant to 11- and 12-year-olds, most of whom were students of color and many of whom were experiencing poverty and homelessness. We believe that it is our moral obligation to teach students in these situations why they are there. It's not a case of laziness or helplessness. Our systems were created to oppress certain groups while privileging others, and this started in ancient times. Over and over, we showed our students how history has repeated itself in various forms. We taught them the foundation that modern day oppression rests on.

We also taught them how loving themselves is the first step to changing oppression. Students were invited to freely and openly talk about their identities and use their identities as a source of power. When we taught a lesson called "Heroes of Color," the warm up question was, "Why are we only focusing on heroes of color?" The students could answer it was equitable to do so because so much of what they had learned before now was about white heroes. Our assessments were generally creative ones in which students could explore the facets of their identities and label them the way they wanted to. For example, when asked their race students responded with things like

Muslim, Vietnamese, Black and Mexican, Somali, etc., and we didn't correct them. Who were we to determine their identity for them? Especially after we had just taught them race is a social construct.

My passion for racial justice and ethnic studies caught the attention of a leader of our education association, Marquita Prinzing. She had recently been hired to create a project for our union focused on racial justice. She recruited me to become part of the advisory committee. Working with Marquita has transformed my life. The "project" has come to be known as The Center for Race and Equity, and it has sustained me and many others in this work. Thanks to Marquita, I met Jon Greenberg who has also had a transformative impact on my life. He recruited me to his quest to get Ethnic Studies into Seattle Public Schools. The rest, as they say, is history — or present.

As I write this personal narrative, I am currently serving as Seattle Public School's Ethnic Studies Program Manager. I'm no longer in the classroom and leaving it was not an easy decision to make. I love my kids, and I love being a teacher. It's the hardest and most fulfilling job I've ever done. I never wanted to be an administrator. I always wanted to be in it with the kids. They're the reason I became a teacher. Yes, I wanted to make a difference, but directly with the kids building relationships and teaching them content they deserve to know. Then, the unthinkable happened. My husband had a heart attack one night at work and never came home.

His name was Brian Gill, and he was the best thing that ever happened to me. He's the reason I was able to finish college after leaving my abusive ex-husband. He's the reason I was able to be so involved in The Center for Race and Equity and the fight for ethnic studies. He would stay home with my child, Elysia. He would cook and clean on the nights I came home too late. He would pay the bills while I went to school full time to get my teaching credentials. He also believed in my work and was my biggest cheerleader. After he died, some of his coworkers wrote condolence notes to me. One of them said, "He was so proud of you and would always talk about how you're a racial justice teacher." I remember once when I was "rabble-rousing," as he called it, he said to me, "The fact that you fight so hard for what you believe in is one of the things I love the most about you." He died February 15, 2018, about one week after my first Teacher of the Year nomination came in. He said, "You know you're going to win."

I gave myself some time and space to deeply mourn and then I rolled up my sleeves and got back to work. It's what he would want me to do. I know he's with me as I move into this next phase of my life. I keep him in my heart to give me strength through the tough moments, and since my new job is to basically break the racist education system, I need a lot of that. When the opportunity came for this position, it was right. I needed a change, and while I am leaving my kids, I am in a better position to improve education for all kids, not just the kids in Seattle.

People around the country are looking to us as we progress. We get requests from people to learn from our program all of the time. I'm in a position to help reform education by learning from and with the people who came before me and setting an example of how community and educator led reform can look.

People say, "You're so strong," "You're an inspiration," or "You're a natural leader." I'm just a woman who is passionate about what I know is right. I know my experiences and how certain moments changed me for the better. I know that I can never go back, so I keep pushing forward. If what I do is inspirational or seen as good leadership, that's a side effect of my drive to prevent young people from having to experience some of the things I did. I'm not strong because of my experiences. I'm angry and motivated because of them. No person should have to live through the things I did. Every person should feel like they are part of a community that is welcoming and inclusive. In an essay about what they learned in school last year, a student wrote, "When students are taught Ethnic Studies, they know that someone like them worked hard and made a change in history. I know this because in school we learn a lot about heroes of color and how they have impacted history. This makes me feel like I belong because I know more about people like me."

As I continue to help shape what Ethnic Studies looks like in Seattle Public Schools, my message is clear. We have the answers. We have the power. We don't need corporate reformers and white saviors. We built our ancient civilizations, invented math and science, survived attempted genocide, and we have the keys to our future. Together we are unstoppable. My story shows it only takes a few dedicated people to come together and build a movement.

There's a Mexican proverb, "Nos enterraron sin saber que tambien somos semillas." How appropriate for this Seed to Apple story? How many people tried to bury me before I blossomed into this apple tree? Will the fruit you bear bury others or help them grow?

Robert Hand
2019 Washington State Teacher of the Year

Mount Vernon High School
Mount Vernon School District

We Are the Champions, My Friends

A teacher discovers his calling is to become the heroes of his own childhood

I wasn't the most disciplined student in school. I didn't really have many goals for the future other than to be successful and happy. I had no idea how I would one day achieve success and happiness, but I had enough faith in myself that I would figure something out. I was a naive kid. But I was lucky to have a few great teachers who helped guide me (eventually) to a career in teaching.

The person I remember the most from my days at Cascade Elementary was my principal, Norm Colon. Mr. Colon was never my teacher, but he felt like one to me. He had the brightest smile and most welcoming spirit. He reminded me of Mr. Rogers. He always took the time to stop and talk to me and ask me how I was doing. I would even stop by the office sometimes just to say "hi" to him. I remember one time we had a substitute, and we had been working on a project with little balloons. Our class had to leave the room to walk somewhere, probably an assembly. For some reason, I got the idea to fill one of the balloons from our project with water and toss it into the crowd as we walked across campus. It was unlike me. I don't know why I did it. It didn't hit anyone, but it landed right next to the substitute. I knew it was wrong as soon as I did it, and I was so afraid I would get in trouble.

At lunch, Mr. Colon approached my table and looked at me with the most disappointed look on his face. I immediately broke down in tears, and he took me to the hall to talk to me. At that moment, I wasn't afraid of what was going to happen to me. I knew I deserved whatever I got. I was crying because I had let Mr. Colon down. He told me he was disappointed because he knew that I was better than that, and then he hugged me and sent me back to lunch. He knew there was nothing more he could say or do that would make me learn more than what I had already learned. I never wanted to let him down like that again.

Like most kids, going to middle school was a big adjustment for me. Because Cedarcrest was a brand-new school, my 6th-grade class would be the first to attend the school for 6th–9th grade. I spent all four years in band with Larry Philpott. There was something about Mr. Philpott that I always admired. He was genuine, he was passionate about music, and he didn't treat us like kids. He had high expectations, and he made me want to try my hardest. I learned how to play a variety of concert percussion instruments in concert band. I showed up before school to take zero-hour jazz band. I went to the band room during lunch to play in a rock band with my friends. I even played drums for the choir across the hall.

I always loved singing, so I'm not sure why I hadn't tried out for choir, too. Until one day when our choir teacher, Mrs. Tripp, stopped me in the hall and said someone told her that I could sing. She asked me why I was holding out on her and made me sing for her. The next thing I knew, I was enrolled in the Select Choir and singing a solo. I ended up taking both band and choir in 9th grade.

Each year at the final band concert, Mr. Philpott would award one 9th-grade student with the Outstanding Band Member Award. It was something I had aspired to over the previous three years, but never thought I'd get. I was convinced another student, a saxophone player and a friend of mine named Bjorn Larsen, was going to get it. I was so excited when Mr. Philpott announced the award at our final concert. I had been selected. I still have the plaque on a shelf in my home office. It was one of my proudest moments in school.

As a high school student, I never planned on going to college. I knew I was unlikely to make it as a professional musician, so I started working during my senior year in high school. I worked for the same company my dad had worked for my whole life. I moved up quickly and, at 19, I moved to Alaska as a manager and helped build and set up a new district of stores for the company. I spent about a year living and working in Alaska before I realized that I was unhappy with the direction my life was going. I was lonely and homesick, so I packed my bags and bought a one-way plane ticket back to Washington. I had no idea where I'd live or work, but I knew I needed to start over. When I returned, I bounced around a lot, sleeping on couches and in my car until I found a job at a music store and an apartment. By the time I was 22, I had worked a number of jobs and learned a lot of difficult life lessons the hard way.

I wasn't living up to the potential my teachers had seen in me and I believed I had. I felt like I was standing in the middle of a marathon, running on a treadmill, while everyone else was passing me by in a blur on their way toward a finish line that I craved but couldn't imagine how to reach. So many people I loved were succeeding in college, and something very powerful occurred to me. I realized, as C.S. Lewis said, "You can't go back and change the beginning, but you can start where you are and change the ending." That really resonated with me. So I enrolled at Edmonds Community College and eventually transferred to Western Washington where I earned my BA in Communication. I didn't have a clear career goal, and the job market was a disaster. I found myself interviewing for the same types of jobs I had been doing before I started in college. I felt defeated. I had come so far, and yet I felt like I was right back where I started. I had earned my college degree, but I also had a new family to support and student loan debt. I didn't want to get back on that same treadmill.

In college, I had a joy that I couldn't quite explain. I loved learning. I loved working as a professor's assistant, helping with lessons and helping students with research papers. I loved education. It suddenly hit me like a ton of bricks. I loved teaching. Teaching was what I was meant to do. Why hadn't I realized it sooner? I was overcome with joy to realize that I had found my passion, but then crippled with fear and uncertainty knowing it meant I would have to return to school in order to pursue it.

I remember being afraid to tell my wife because I didn't know how she would respond. I knew this was something I needed to do, but I had no idea how it would be possible. We went for a walk on Centennial Trail, and I mustered up the courage to say it: "I want to become a teacher." It took her by surprise, but she didn't complain at all. She thought about it for a minute, and then she asked me why.

I knew I wanted to teach because I wanted to do for other students what Mr. Colon, Mr. Philpott, and Mrs. Tripp had done for me. I wanted to be the kind of teacher who really knows their students the way Mr. Colon knew me and my character. I wanted to set the bar high like Mr. Philpott, and I wanted my students to know I saw they were capable like Mrs. Tripp. The additional master's degree and 50 extra credits in Family and Consumer Sciences were a challenge to be sure, but so worth it to educate young people and help them realize their full potential 30 years after Mr. Colon had reminded me of mine. I love my job.

Susan Douglas
Northeast ESD 101 Regional Teacher of the Year

Almira Elementary
Almira School District

A Voice From the Corner
Relevance transforms a reluctant student into a leader

 t was the first period of the first day of a new year. Each of our 8th-grade students were required to be in my service-learning classroom (even though we called it an elective). Many had clues to class expectations based on a reputation I have as an instructor. Having class first thing in the morning when you are fourteen is a motivational challenge, but on this first period of the first day in a new year, all 8th graders were present. One student entered my classroom dressed in a way that gave me the impression he wanted to disappear. In his dark and heavy clothing, he found a seat on the edge of the group. What he was about to teach me in this new school year would bring me to a paradigm shift in my approach to teaching students.

As he sat in the corner of the room, I began to deliver my "hook" for the class. We started our whole group discussion with an inspirational video of how a 12-year-old was making a difference in India and moved into who were our mentors, who inspired us. My student in the corner did not participate.

We passed out student journals for the semester. The students would have daily prompts, and they could write or draw responses. Whatever was displayed on the pages was confidential, and as I encouraged, sharing out was always their choice. I used this as a means of developing trust and consistency with my students, as well as building their voice in a safe environment. At fourteen a room full of peers can be very intimidating. Establishing a relationship and dialogue with each student is especially challenging at this age, but also paramount in making the journey to the risk taking I was asking them to do.

The students would be delving into and challenging their mindsets. Starting with a great deal of self-reflection, they would build understanding of who they were in their families, peer groups, school, communities, and the larger world. I was asking them to take this knowledge and step up into civic awareness and engagement.

Initially, I saw high absences from my student in the corner. His journal entries challenged the rest of his class (on paper only); their assumptions, their expressions, and their judgments.

He wrote that he wore certain clothes to intentionally confront the norms in our school. He wanted to be different, and kind of be in their face about it. He didn't feel like he belonged, and his words had a vast amount of pain and disappointment in them. As we conversed via notebook paper back and forth, I listened and validated his unique life experiences. I also assured him that he did belong, especially in my classroom. I encouraged him to stay the course and show up for school. His service-learning experience was about removing obstacles that kept him from discovering passions and finding purpose.

After about a month of journal entries and activities in our class time, he began to open up more. He'd be the last one working on the journal entry each day, and eagerly wait for me to hand them out at the beginning of class the next morning so he could read my response. I never imagined the power that this format in working with students would have. Many days I was overwhelmed with their stories and reflections. The struggles of middle school students are legitimate. Some face so many challenges just surviving the incredible episodes life has given them.

Part of my expectation in the semester was for the class to choose a project as a group. The students in this particular semester had a reputation for not being very academic. Their lives were full of adverse experiences, poverty, and judgments. Many people expected less engagement and fewer accomplishments from them. Yet, these were the students who wrote their hearts on the pages in their journals to me each day.

They chose to take on the school's Veterans' Day project. As a major public event, it was a huge responsibility. When we began to speak about the project, the young man in the corner moved to the center of the room. Standing at the white board, I could not keep up with their ideas. They visualized the day with details and activities that poured from them freely. The excitement in the room elevated every student. By the end of our brain storming, the students were standing around me, picking up markers, and taking over the lead.

They researched and discussed post-traumatic stress disorder for veterans, interviewed local veterans, and created a plan bigger than any public event I have ever held. They adopted an organization that serves wounded veterans for the program. The coolest part? These students were in charge. It was for me a transformational experience. I could barely keep up.

The student who started in the corner on an August day was now a leader in the project. He took over the huge artwork display. He coordinated with other classrooms for student materials. Using paper, he created a tree that would take up half the gym wall for the event, writing parts of the Declaration of Independence, Constitution, Bill of Rights, and Emancipation Proclamation on its trunk and strong branches. When other students asked me what needed to be done, I redirected them to him. He delegated tasks and inspired them. He was a lead for the times students came in on Friday evenings and Saturday mornings to complete the project.

His demeanor had changed. His attendance was up. He came to school early. He was connected. He not only came to understand that he belonged, he understood that he made a significant difference. His artistic talent filled a school gymnasium and touched the hearts of community members. After a day full of events for our younger students and an evening program that brought those in attendance to tears, all of the service-learning students stood inches taller in their self-confidence and understanding of their importance as members of our community.

The young voice from the corner had taken me on a journey in this semester. He helped me as a teacher fully grasp the importance of making all of education relevant to our students' lives. I realized the depth of difference we can make for all of students, regardless of content areas. It isn't just in a service-learning project, but in math, science, and language arts that students need to be expressing themselves and actively engaged in their learning. As educators, our instruction should be student focused. My student changed when he felt heard, respected for his individuality, and given space to grow into his capacity in that moment.

Witnessing his journey (and his continued success) challenged me to make my math and science classes more relevant to our students. In the years since this experience, I've been teaching elementary students. I continue to see similar transformations in students at the earliest age when they have an opportunity to express their unique perspective of the world through authentic and meaningful experiences.

This young man's voice was a catalyst that encouraged me to take risks and step outside the box in science and math. With the trust and support of my administrator, I developed new programs that pivot from traditional classrooms where students learn of the world to empowering students to learn from and alongside their community. Even at the earliest ages learning about and being involved in the community around them can change student perspective. They begin to see themselves as important members of our community. They realize there is more to their world and that the people in it have a wealth of knowledge to share.

Students began to learn about these people using real math and science. The new mentors were people they saw every day: custodian, transportation manager, and school cook. Students learned how we manage air quality in our building, conducted science investigations, and made recommendations. They converted recipes from the cafeteria to single servings and calculated out their favorite recipe to feed all the students in the building. We realized while studying mining, that our custodian was an expert in our midst. The class discovered that learning the stories of others leads to learning from others. These other "teachers" were excited to take this journey alongside them.

I added more layers by inviting first responders to be our audience in the capstone projects of earthquakes, hurricanes, floods, and tornadoes. It gave students a greater purpose in preparing their models, public service announcements, and presentations. These were men and women they knew and admired. They were now in their classroom and expanding their learning experiences.

In all these settings, and more like it, my students grew beyond anyone's expectations. I grew as an educator watching the profound ramifications of opening the doors to my classrooms and elevating student voice. Curricula come in a box with a set of instructions. Students don't. They need us to be creative, compassionate, and courageous in delivering an educational experience that brings meaning to their lives and empowers them in their world.

Michael Clinton
ESD 105 Regional Teacher of the Year

White Swan High School
Mt. Adams School District

Building a Bridge

Supporting Native students who suffer abuse requires deep cross-cultural understanding and collaboration

I offer greetings to the People of the Big River. I am a white man. I teach your children. There are many of us, white teachers, who want to learn and understand your ways — to help teach your children what is important to you. You have taught me much about your oral traditions. In my science classroom, we talk about the forest, the eel, the salmon, and the wild horses. I teach your children what I know, and they teach me what they know. Sometimes our learning fits into what my government says your children should know about science. But often, we learn about what matters on the reservation and in their lives.

As part of my mission to integrate your culture into my teaching, I use nature and the environment as my classroom. Every year I take students, along with many others, on a two-week field trip. During this trip, we camp in tents in various areas along the Big River and its many tributaries. We visit different tribes. We explore their ways and the challenges they face. On this field trip we ask: How can science combine with traditions to solve problems? How can science bring back the salmon and eel or solve the wild horse problem? Your children learn a lot about these challenges, about the ways of other tribes, and what they can do to enact change.

As you can imagine, during those two weeks on the road with people of many different backgrounds, completely dependent on one another, we bond. We build trust. We can also get on each other's nerves a bit. This is where the sharing circles with our host tribes come in.

At these sharing circles, we talk a lot about our lives. It is a safe place. For me, sometimes I share about my family, how much I love them, and how I do not get the chance to see them enough. Sometimes I share how grateful I am for the students on the trip. I tell them how I grew up poor and how I found my passion in teaching.

The children share, too. They talk about the things that are important to them. They talk about loved ones they miss "back home." Sometimes, they talk about how they enjoyed our camping trip more than others they have been on. They talk about what they have learned from the other tribes, lands, and traditions. Sometimes students share more than I expect. Sometimes they share stories about abuse. And this is where I need your help.

My government requires that I report when students tell me they have been abused or have suicidal thoughts. I do this, and sometimes I am able to get the child help. But too often that help is temporary. The child still needs more help than I can give them, and often it seems to my white eyes that my help is not enough.

Talking about abuse is not easy, but I believe it is a conversation that we need to have. Whenever teachers hear of abuse of any kind, we report it. We know there are other ways to help, but many of us do not know how. You have taught me much about your first foods and The Big River. I think, perhaps, what we need now is for you to teach us how your communities deal with abuse — with respect to the survivor and the offender both.

I know that white institutions could benefit from these conversations, and I think Native communities could, too. On one hand, a better understanding for how specifically white institutions, like schools and teachers, can help support Native abuse survivors. On the other, a better understanding for what cultural traditions Native communities already have for dealing with abuse. I believe understanding and bringing these together will help us come to some better way of reporting, enforcing, and helping the survivors of abuse.

This is not easy to talk about, but I believe it is important. The children we all care about need us to find a better way of addressing this issue — to build a bridge of understanding between white institutions and your cultural traditions. I hope this message will begin more conversations. I hope you will visit our school, and I invite you into my classroom. I keep your stories, words, and ideas with me as I teach, but they are no substitute for your presence.

I know it may take time for our relationship to grow. In the meantime, I will continue to include your traditions in my teaching and do everything I can to make sure your children are safe and have the tools and opportunities to live their best lives.

Kristine Mars
ESD 123 Regional Teacher of the Year

Lincoln Elementary
Kennewick School District

The Road From Trauma To Hope

A teacher's personal tragedy gives her a window into the emotional lives of her students

C hampions never quit" was frequently heard rolling off the tongue of Bob Mars, a teacher, mentor, and coach in the Kiona-Benton School district for 15 years. This was his message of hope to his students and athletes; a message that I carry forward as his widow. In September of 2004, Bob was murdered at his school by two troubled teens following the season opener football game.

Following Bob's death, I felt a calling to carry on his legacy as a teacher. I needed to return the kindness the community had bestowed upon my family in our darkest days. There was a sense of duty burning within me to make a change. I returned to college, earned my degree in education, and started my journey as a teacher.

In September 2014 I was a second year, 2nd-grade teacher, ready to begin a new school year. The air was electric with excitement and hope as I greeted each child who attended "Sneak Peek," our school's version of a pre-open house event. There were 31 students on my roster — a rather large class size at the primary level — and I pondered how I would meet each child's needs.

Roughly half of my students and their families attended that night. My principal noted the numbers were actually a good turn out, but I felt defeated by the results. During the summer, I had mailed home letters to the parents and guardians. A personal postcard was sent to each student. Building relationships with my students and their families, even before school begins, lays the foundation for the school year. It was clear to me that I had not done enough.

School started, and I had a rough bunch. Several students had behavioral issues, others were well below grade-level, and a handful had chronic attendance issues. One student in particular tugged at my heartstrings: Bruno. His family struggled with poverty, and as a result was homeless. Bruno exhibited behavioral issues, was identified as oppositional defiant, and was falling behind his peers in achieving his learning goals. But, when Bruno smiled, he stole my heart; not just a little piece, but he swallowed it up, completely.

Bruno was what research refers to as a student in trauma. The CDC-Kaiser Permanente ACE study (Adverse Childhood Experiences, aka children in trauma) reports that about two-thirds of all adults have at least one adverse childhood experience. Another study from the National Survey of Children's Health reports that approximately 68 percent of children 0–17 years old had experienced one or more ACEs. These adverse experiences include neglect, abuse, and the absence of a parent due to divorce, death, or mental illness. The effects can include behavioral issues, impaired learning, and even long-term health issues.

There were several adverse childhood experiences that I knew had affected Bruno, and there were likely others I never learned. I worked tirelessly to build a relationship with Bruno and his family. I connected them with as many resources and supports as I could. At Christmastime, I elicited help from my friends through social media to shower his family with love, food, and gifts. My friends did not disappoint with their generosity for complete strangers. In return, Bruno's entire family came together and signed a beautiful Christmas card, which I treasure to this day.

Bruno continued to struggle. He had outbursts and was withdrawn. I doubted my teaching abilities, carried home guilt that I was not doing enough to help him, and cried many tears for this sweet 7-year-old boy. Most days Bruno refused to do classwork, often swinging his arm across his desk, scattering all the pages through the air before falling to the floor in a mess. It was symbolic of his life. The hand he had been dealt was unfair, but it did not have to define him. I whispered that to him many times. He needed to know that there was still hope.

That school year taught me many things about my students and myself. I reflected on how the trauma of Bob's murder had impacted my return to college. It was difficult to concentrate. I experienced anxiety. There were days I could barely motivate myself to get out of bed, let alone take on an entire day of activities.

I reflected on the toll it took on my two young sons. The amount of school they missed and the daily struggle to keep it together was overwhelming. Things that had previously been easy for them, for us, now seemed impossible. One misspoken word could illicit a complete meltdown.

I reflected on how Bruno was in survival mode: fight or flight was his norm. How could it not be? In addition, how could I, as his teacher, expect him to "perform" as a student? He did not know where his next meal was coming from. Where would he rest his head that night? When would his dad return from California?

Bruno forever changed how I approach my students. That little boy taught me to look at each child through a different lens. Our students are not test scores. Their learning is not a performance. They are individuals who bring so much more to the classroom than we can see. Sometimes, like Bruno, they come to us with experiences that no 7-year-old should have to deal with. They need a loving adult to show them there is hope.

Homelessness and other issues continue to plague Bruno and his family. When he was in 5th grade, his niece was in my class, which opened a new line of communication with him. Bruno was at yet another school, struggling with daily expectations. Near the end of his 5th-grade year, he was suspended for fighting. On the day of his suspension, imagine my surprise when he showed up at my classroom door! We shared a hug, and he whispered, "I love you, Mrs. Mars." In that moment, Bruno let me know that I was his beacon of hope.

Bruno is not an isolated case. Children in trauma are in every classroom, in every school, in every district across our state, and across our nation. My own children were students in trauma. I became an adult student in trauma, and to this day Bruno continues to be a student in trauma.

What I learned from Bruno and what I believe he learned from me, is that given the proper tools and pathways there is always hope. Bruno is learning that his education can open the doors of his future. I learned that being a teacher provided me with hope for future generations. It also allowed me to be Bruno's champion, a role that honors Bob.

Ryan Healy

Capital Region ESD 113 Regional Teacher of the Year

Ridgeline Middle School
Yelm School District

Take Care of Yourself

One small gesture can save a life

Little things are important. The small interactions and behaviors that we share with the people around us shape our world. In schools, these interactions can transform students' lives for the better or for the worse. I didn't always understand this. One brave student taught me the importance of owning my words and actions and helped me learn that being available is maybe the most important thing a teacher can do for a student.

I'll never forget that day. One of my students stayed after class. They waited until everyone had gone and when the room was clear, they began to cry. I immediately asked if they were okay. Seeing that they weren't, I offered to give them a hug. The student accepted and squeezed me like their life depended on it. When they finally stepped back, the student pulled up their sleeve and showed me where they had been hurting themselves. And then they said, "Mr. Healy, I've been considering doing more than that."

All of the alarm bells in my brain started to ring at once. We walked down to the counselor together. The counselor and I were able to get support for that student during a very difficult and confusing time for them.

Two weeks after this interaction, I did an activity near the end of class called the four H's. It's a connection activity where we ask students to find four different people in the room and do one of four things with that person: give them a handshake, a high-five, a hand hug, or (if they feel comfortable) a hug. Then, on the way out the door, they can choose one of those connections, and we will do that together. I'll even give them a hug if that is what they want.

The student who had stayed after class two weeks before came up and asked to give me a hug. We hugged. I said, "take care of yourself."

Several months passed. During one week, I asked the students in class to write thank you notes to practice expressing their gratitude to people who were important in their lives. On the last day of that week, during the last moments of class, I looked up and saw the same student drop a letter on my desk. When the letter landed, it made a thud. As a teacher, when you get a letter that makes a thud, it's either going to say something really amazing or something really difficult. This letter was both.

After everyone left, I opened the letter. I started to read it at my desk, and I immediately began to cry. You see, the letter explained that the day we had done the four H's, my student had planned to go home and take their own life. The student eloquently explained that in the moment of contemplating taking their life, all they could think about were the four words I had said, "take care of yourself." They said that in that moment those words helped them understand that they had to come back on Monday. They wanted to see me, and they knew they had more to do with their life.

As soon as I finished reading the letter, I went to speak with our counselor to check in on our student and to process the difficult set of emotions I was experiencing. All was good for our student, and I was forever changed.

The thing is, I didn't realize I had said those words to that student on that day. I had said the phrase "take care of yourself" to students probably hundreds of times. Although I always truly meant those words and the kindness that came with them, I didn't fully comprehend how important they could be for any single kid. To this day, I say those words to my students often, but now they clearly have a different meaning. They remind me that all teachers have the opportunity to change the lives of their students with things as simple as words.

I have learned that the little things I do every day, the small interactions with every kid in my building are where the real impacts are happening in their lives. The little things are actually the big things.

About Teacher of the Year

Since 1963, the Washington State Teacher of the Year program has selected one outstanding educator annually to serve as the Washington State Teacher of the Year. The Teacher of the Year is selected from a slate of up to 9 regional candidates representing Washington's nine Educational Service Districts (ESDs) and including Tribal Schools. In 1963, 1970, 2007, 2013, and 2018, the state program garnered national attention when Elmon Ousley of Bellevue School District, Johnnie T. Dennis of Walla Walla School District, Andrea Peterson of Granite Falls School District, Jeff Charbonneau of Zillah School District, and Mandy Manning of Spokane School District, respectively, were each selected as the National Teacher of the Year.

Anyone can nominate someone for Teacher of the Year. Nominated teachers complete a written application and enter the regional selection process through their ESDs. Each ESD recommends a Regional Teacher of the Year to the state program. Regional Teachers of the Year undergo a rigorous state selection that includes a written application, presentation, and panel interview. The State Teacher of the Year is selected by a committee made up of diverse educators, families, students, and education stakeholders. Teachers of the Year:

- Have the respect of their community.

- Are knowledgeable in their fields and guide students of all backgrounds and abilities to achieve excellence.

- Collaborate with colleagues, students, and families to create school cultures of respect and success.

- Deliberately connect the classroom and key stakeholders to foster strong communities at large.

- Demonstrate leadership and innovation in and outside of the classroom walls that embodies lifelong learning.

- Express themselves in engaging and effective ways.